To The Herndons,

    Be blessed my Beloveds,

        Aunt Naida

BACK TO EDEN

LIVING UNDER THE ORIGINAL BLESSING

NAIDA M. PARSON, PH.D.

Naida M. Parson, PhD

Copyright © 2017 Naida M. Parson, Ph.D..

All rights reserved. No part of this book may be used or reproduced by any means, graphic, electronic, or mechanical, including photocopying, recording, taping or by any information storage retrieval system without the written permission of the author except in the case of brief quotations embodied in critical articles and reviews.

Unless otherwise specified, scripture quotations marked NIV are taken from the Holy Bible, New International Version. NIV. Copyright 1973, 1978, 1984 by International Bible Society. Used by permission of Zondervan. All rights reserved.

Scripture quotations marked KJV are from the Holy Bible, King James Version (Authorized Version). First published in 1611. Quoted from the KJV Classic Reference Bible, Copyright 1983 by The Zondervan Corporation. WestBow Press books may be ordered through booksellers or by contacting:

This book is a work of non-fiction. Unless otherwise noted, the author and the publisher make no explicit guarantees as to the accuracy of the information contained in this book and in some cases, names of people and places have been altered to protect their privacy.

I Don't Know How To Stop by Naida M. Parson, Ph.D. © 2015

WestBow Press
A Division of Thomas Nelson & Zondervan
1663 Liberty Drive
Bloomington, IN 47403
www.westbowpress.com
1 (866) 928-1240

Because of the dynamic nature of the Internet, any web addresses or links contained in this book may have changed since publication and may no longer be valid. The views expressed in this work are solely those of the author and do not necessarily reflect the views of the publisher, and the publisher hereby disclaims any responsibility for them.

Any people depicted in stock imagery provided by Thinkstock are models, and such images are being used for illustrative purposes only.
Certain stock imagery © Thinkstock.

ISBN: 978-1-5127-8624-8 (sc)
ISBN: 978-1-5127-8625-5 (e)

Library of Congress Control Number: 2017906928

Print information available on the last page.

WestBow Press rev. date: 7/20/2017

This book is dedicated to everyone who has ever stepped foot in New Antioch Christian Fellowship where we are People Focused and Purpose Driven. You have been a church who displays that everybody matters to God….Everybody. You are a Christian community who speaks to the greatness in all of us and I have been blessed to be your Senior Pastor. So I speak to all of us when I say what God spoke to humankind at the very beginning and what His Word still speaks today. Be fruitful, my beloveds. Multiply. Fill your lives to capacity. Subdue your world and have dominion over it. I love you with my life.

CONTENTS

Introduction ix

Chapter 1   *Parah!* Be Fruitful 1

Chapter 2   *Rabah!* Multiply 13

Chapter 3   *Male!* Fill to Capacity 21

Chapter 4   *Kabash!* Subdue 31

Chapter 5   *Radah!* Have Dominion 43

Epilogue   Let's Get Back to Eden 53

INTRODUCTION

And God said, "Let us make man in Our image, after Our likeness: and let them have dominion over the fish of the sea, and over the fowl of the air, and over the cattle, and over all the earth, and over every creeping thing that creepeth upon the earth." So God created man in His own image, in the image of God created He him; male and female created He them. And God blessed them, and God said unto them, "Be fruitful, (parah) and multiply (rabah) and replenish the earth (male) and subdue it (kabash) and have dominion (radah) over the fish of the sea, and over the fowl of the air, and over every living thing that moveth upon the earth."(Genesis 1:26—28 KJV)

On the sixth day of creation, as God hovered over the man and the woman He had made in His image and after His likeness, He blessed them. God uttered five powerful words. Five blessings. Five abilities. Five areas of authority. This blessing gave to the newly created humankind the capacity for a full and prosperous life. He didn't just make the man and the woman and then leave them on their own. The Bible says He blessed them. The Hebrew word for blessing often means to speak well of, or over, the one being blessed. So God spoke well of them and gave them the ability to fulfill the purpose for which He created them.

Humankind still has that capacity today. We still have the blessing God spoke to all humankind. This five-fold blessing gives us the ability to do what we were created to do. In spite of our fall, and in spite of our sin, there are things that God spoke during creation that are still in effect today. For example, He spoke to the light, and there has been light ever since. He spoke to the sky, and there has been sky ever since. He spoke to plants and trees and animals, and there has been life on planet earth ever since. And He spoke blessing to the man and the woman, and our ability to perform that word has been released ever since.

God has led me to share this teaching on the original blessing that we were given back in the Garden of Eden. Sin complicated the blessing. Sin brought curses into our lives. But, sin did not cancel out the blessing. Especially, now that Christ has redeemed us from the curse of sin, we can claim and live out our original blessing. We are to continue to be fruitful and multiply, replenish, subdue, and have dominion.

The original Hebrew words are *parah*, *rabah*, *male* (pronounced maw-lay), *kabash*, and *radah*. In this book, we will look at them one by one and hopefully increase your faith and confidence to experience them in your life. It's a blessed lifestyle and it belongs to you.

CHAPTER 1

Parah! Be Fruitful

And God blessed them, and God said
unto them, "Be fruitful (*parah*)..."

If you are tired of living life with nothing to show for it, this is the blessing for you! God declared that you have the ability to be fruitful. You have the capacity to be fruitful. The Hebrew word *parah* has multiple meanings, and though correct hermeneutical exegesis (applying the strict principles of biblical interpretation) would suggest that the author may only have intended one meaning, the Bible is alive. Many biblical words unfold multiple meanings that can be used for inspiration's sake. Each of the blessings God pronounced on humankind has layers of powerful abilities all enclosed in one word. The first word applied to humankind is *parah*! Be fruitful!

BE PRODUCTIVE

The first meaning of the word *parah* that we will explore is to "be productive." As God blessed humankind, He spoke out of the heavens to be productive! We are not to live a lazy lifestyle that does not produce anything. God has an attitude with things that take up space and resources, but do not produce. This was quite evident in the life of Jesus Christ, who is the image of God, the Father. Jesus cursed a fig tree that was taking up space and resources, but was not being productive.

> Early in the morning, as Jesus was on his way back to the city, he was hungry. Seeing a fig tree by the road, he went up to it, but found nothing on it except leaves. Then he said to it, "May you never bear fruit again!" Immediately the tree withered. (Matthew 21:18—19 NIV)

Jesus also told a parable about another fig tree.

> Then he told this parable: "A man had a fig tree growing in his vineyard, and he went to look for fruit on it, but did not find any. So he said to the man who took care of the vineyard, 'For three years now I've been coming to look for fruit on this fig tree and haven't found any. Cut it down! Why should it use up the soil?'" (Luke 13:6—7 NIV)

Jesus again taught a parable about a servant who did not produce.

> "His master replied, 'You wicked, lazy servant! So you knew that I harvest where I have not sown and gather where I have not scattered seed? Well then, you should have put my money on deposit with the bankers, so that when I returned I would have received it back with interest. So take the bag of gold from him and give it to the one who has ten bags.' For whoever has will be given more, and they will have an abundance. Whoever does not have, even what they have will be taken from them. And throw that worthless servant outside, into the darkness, where there will be weeping and gnashing of teeth." (Matthew 25:26—30 NIV)

One tree was cursed. Another tree cut down. An unproductive servant was thrown into torment. God definitely seems to have an attitude about things that do not produce. You were designed to be productive, and I don't want to condemn you if you have not been up to this point. I want to inspire you. I want to remind you. I want to fill you with faith and expectation. God has spoken a blessing over you, and you have the ability and the capacity to *be productive*.

The reason we call fruits and vegetables "produce" is because they are the final product of the work of the tree or plant. If the tree is an apple tree, everything needed to produce apples is surging through that tree. When everything does what it is designed to do from the root through the branches, the final result, the "produce," will be apples.

You are capable of producing fruit. That fruit will come from whatever is surging through you. Whatever that is would be from your purpose. The purpose of an apple tree is to produce apples. The purpose of a fig tree is to produce figs. So whatever kind of person you are, whatever is in you and surging through you, that is your purpose—and it shall produce fruit.

So if you were a tree, what is it that you produce? What is in you? What is surging through you? What is working its way out from the inside of you? Whatever that is, that is your purpose. Philippians 2:13 says that *it is God who works in you to will and to act in order to fulfill His good purpose.* When God has a purpose for your life, He places that purpose inside of you. Your job is to work out of you what is placed in you.

> Therefore, my dear friends, as you have always obeyed—not only in my presence, but now much more in my absence—continue to work out your salvation with fear and trembling. (Philippians 2:12 NIV)

What do you have to show for your work? What can you point to? What can you present? What do you have to show for your time on planet earth? If you have not seen fruit come from what has been placed in you, then remember that you are living under this blessing. Pray in agreement with God's will for your life. Know that He has something raging inside of you. Something surging through you like the apple tree has all the makings of multiple apples surging through it from the roots to the branches. Declare that fruitfulness will come forth. You will not live life unproductive. *Parah*! *Be fruitful* means to *be productive*.

BE INCREASED

The Hebrew word can also be translated as "be increased." There is more to you than this. Whatever you are right now, whoever you are right now, there is more *to* you and there is more *in* you than this! There in the Garden of Eden, God looked at the man and woman before Him. There were only two of them, but He saw billions of them and spoke what He saw. Be increased!

When He looks at you, there may be a house, a car, a job, a few kids, a few dollars, a poem, a song, or a sermon or two. But what He actually sees are houses, books, souls saved, college degrees, businesses, multiple bank accounts, ministries, healings by the hundreds, preaching to thousands, recordings, songs, leadership, and careers. God created us with the ability to become more than what we see at any given time. Just like a rubber band is designed to stretch, we were designed to increase. We were designed to become more, to be more, and to do more. There is so much in you that He sees, so He speaks to it to come forth when He says *parah*!

You already have increase in you, but the blessing from God brings it forth. For the man and woman God created, *parah* was meant for them to increase in number. For us, this blessing should inspire personal increase as well. There is such potential for increase in you financially, spiritually, intellectually and socially—in every area. *Parah!* Be increased! Lay before God every area of your life. Lay before Him every talent, gift, and ability that you have. Lay before Him everything that He has given you as a blessing, and expect that the word already spoken over you will bring increase. Each year you should expect to be more, know more, and achieve more than what you have been, known, or achieved up until now. Don't settle for a mediocre, unsatisfactory life. Don't settle for a life where you are barely making it. You were designed to increase!

GROW...GROW UP...GROW OUT

So far, the blessing of *parah* is to be fruitful, to be productive, and to increase. The next translation of the word is "to grow." You don't have to stay at the same level that you have been all this time. Grow! Are you praying better, fasting more effectively, preaching under a more powerful anointing, or singing with more purpose and greater skill as the years go on? Do you have a deeper relationship with Christ? Are you handling money better this year? Are you a wiser parent, a more loving wife, or a stronger husband? Are you a better quality person as every year goes by?

This blessing over your life gives you the ability to grow.

You have the capacity to grow! Don't let the next five years find you in the same place you are right now. There is no time for regret or pining over what could have been. Just take it from where you are right now and grow! Growth is positive change. Each year should bring some positive change into your life. You should be learning things each year that cause you to perform differently. Each experience should teach you something you didn't know before. You were not designed to be stagnant. You were designed to grow.

You have the capacity to grow up. Few things irritate me more than encountering people I haven't seen in twenty years and they haven't changed a bit. They have the same hang-ups, they have the same insecurities, and they are on the same spiritual level as they were the last time I saw them. They have no financial gain and are using the same excuses for their lack of progress. It is disheartening, especially because we have been given the capacity to grow up. It is in our DNA to mature emotionally, and spiritually, as much as it is in us to grow up physically. So if you are still having little-girl issues—grow up! If you are still angry over little-boy hurts—grow up! If you're still looking for momma's love instead of looking to give love to some other searching heart, then grow up! If you are looking for daddy's attention instead of encouraging someone else and pulling greatness out of them, then grow up! You don't have to stay stagnant and immature and plagued by the demons of your past. *Parah!* Grow up.

You have the capacity to grow out. Everything in creation was designed to grow out. That means growing beyond the original limited space. God made plants to grow out. They start small in a patch of dirt and grow larger taking up much more space. Trees grow out from the root to the branches, and both continue to grow out and away from their original place. The direction of growth is not inward but outward. Humankind is under a blessing that gives us the ability to grow out. We should be growing out of our original place in life. Our gifts and talents should be developing so much so that they begin to impact people outside of our original sphere of influence. Whatever we do should be growing out to more people, more venues, more cities, and more resources. We were designed to grow out.

BRANCH OFF

Connected to growing out is another meaning of the word *parah*. *Parah* also means "to branch off." There should be something branching off from you. For Adam and Eve, they were to have children who were to branch off, and they were to have other children who were to branch off, and then they were to have more children. For us, we are to branch off in our purpose and life work. The fruit of our ministry should branch off into other ministries, which in turn should bear fruit. The people who are saved through our testimonies should go out and save other souls. The family you raised in the Lord should grow up and raise their family in the Lord, who in turn should raise the next generation in the Lord. The business you start should branch off and become a franchise. Your program should branch off into other programs that impact a greater number of people in other places.

A fruitful tree has more than one branch. Each branch has the capacity to bear fruit. It does not have to toil to do that. Branching is part of what it was created to do. Unlike trees, we don't let the flow of what is in us just naturally do what it is designed to do. So we have to remind ourselves that God has given us the ability to branch off. We have to be intentional about it. We have to walk down that road, open that door, and take that opportunity. When we believe the blessing to branch off is spoken over us, we can expand and increase without fear of failure. *Parah*! Be fruitful. Be productive. Increase. Grow. Branch off.

FLOURISH

The next meaning of this word is "to flourish." This speaks to explosive, constant, and healthy growth. This is not just quantity, this is quality. Not only are you blessed to be fruitful, but your fruit is to be good, healthy, and constant. What good has come out of your life? What good has come out of your home, your ministry, your business, or your gifts? God commands you to flourish!

Jesus said, in John 15, that your fruit should remain. It should have lasting effects and be good for something in the long run. As a pastor, I don't just want members to join our congregation—that would be increase. I want them to be born again, to be changed, to walk in purpose, to grow spiritually, and to be able to win others for Jesus Christ—that would be flourishing. You don't just want a big savings account to go with your retirement check—that would be increase. You want stocks, income growth accounts, several streams of income, property, an inheritance for your children's children, along with health, and a spiritual legacy that springs from your intimate, long-standing relationship with God—that would be flourishing. God has given you the capacity to flourish in whatever your purpose happens to be. You can have rapid, constant, and healthy growth in business, in ministry, in relationships, in education, or in whatever you endeavor. *Parah*! This blessing has been spoken over your life by your Creator. It is time for you to walk into it. Claim it confidently, and push until you see it manifested in your life.

REPRODUCE THE SAME KIND IN SUCCESSIVE GENERATIONS

As God spoke this word over humankind, He had also spoken this word over every living thing. In expanded form, *parah* means to produce an offspring, or produce a harvest of the same kind in a successive generation. In the blessing of *parah*, God gives all living things, and especially humankind, the ability and the capacity to reproduce themselves—to produce a "harvest" of the same kind in the next generation. For us, it means more than having children. It also means that we have been blessed to be able to reproduce our purpose, our knowledge, our wisdom, our authority, our business sense, or our perspective into a new generation, both spiritually and naturally.

You have not fulfilled this part of your blessing if it all dies with you. If you are a teacher, there should be some other teachers coming that are just like you. If you are a great parent, there should be some great parents coming behind you that are just like you. If you are a prolific preacher, there should be some prolific preachers coming that were mentored by you. If you are an entrepreneur, there should be some businessmen and businesswomen who have been nurtured by you that are coming in the next generation. If you are an intercessor, a giver, or at the very least, a loving Christian, you should be reproducing an offspring or harvest of the same kind in a successive generation. Be fruitful! Produce an offspring of people in the next generation with your same kind of passion and purpose.

ABUNDANCE

Lastly, this powerful first blessing suggests "abundance." Everything mentioned previously should be produced in abundance. Fruitfulness, productivity, increase, growth, branching off, flourishing, and reproducing are all done in abundance. This word means that there will be a whole lot of all of the above. Jesus said, "I come that you may have life and that you will have it more abundantly." (see John 10) Paul gave the declaration: "now unto Him that is able to do exceeding abundantly above all that we ask or think according to the power that works in us." (Ephesians 3:20 KJV) God has blessed us, and is working in us, to make us fruitful in abundance. You are to produce and reproduce in abundance.

You don't have to live an unproductive life. You don't have to be at the same level year after year. Your income, your influence, your accomplishment, your ministry, and your personal life has a blessing over it that causes you to be fruitful in abundance. It is time for you to walk in this blessing. You have to believe that it is for you, that it has been spoken over you as well, and that it is still in effect. If you don't believe it, you will let opportunities slip away from you. You will sit, when you should be moving out. You will shy away, when you should be aggressive. You will be discouraged, when you should hang in there and wait for the blessing to do the work. *Parah*! Be fruitful, be productive, increase, grow, branch off, flourish, produce offspring of the same kind in abundance. And God blessed them, and said unto them, *parah*!

CHAPTER 2

Rabah! Multiply

And God blessed them, and God said unto them,
"Be fruitful (*parah*), and multiply (*rabah*)…"

BECOME GREAT

This word translated "multiply" means to be, or to become, great. It means to grow great. Imagine God looking down on the man and woman He created. He wanted to give them the capacity to be what He designed them to be. So, He speaks these words out of His mouth that cannot return to Him void. That means that every word God speaks has to accomplish the purpose for which He sent it out. He says to them, rather He commands them, to *parah*! Be fruitful! And then *rabah*! Multiply, become great, be great, or grow great! Be fruitful already meant to grow in number and in kind. Now He says, don't just grow, but grow until you hit great. Be great in this earth. This is your world, so be great in it.

With this blessing spoken over your life, why are you not

doing big things? God has not only blessed you to be productive, to be reproductive, to flourish, and to grow, but to do it so consistently that you become great. You should be doing big things! You were not designed for mediocrity. Whatever your big thing is, find your greatness in it. It may not be on someone else's level, but are you a great you? Is there more in you than this? There is a blessing over your life. It is the original blessing that gives you the capacity to become great. So why are you not doing big things?

BECOME MANY

For Adam and Eve, as the first representatives of humankind, this word *rabah* meant mostly to be, or to become, many, to make many, or to become numerous. God expected to start with the two of them, and then look again and see fifty of them, and then look again and see fifty thousand, and then look again and see fifty million. Adam and Eve did just that—they became many, they became numerous. The same blessing is on you. Whatever you put your hands to should become many. It should become numerous. If its money you are called to make, and God opens the door for you to make $50, when He looks again it should be $50,000. If you keep the $50,000 under the blessing, and making money is your call, your gift, and your destiny, then He should look again and see $50,000,000.

If souls for the Kingdom is your purpose, call, and anointing, then when you win five people to Christ and God looks again, there should be fifty people added to the Kingdom. If you keep that result under the blessing, it should multiply until it becomes great, until it becomes many, and when God looks again, there should be fifty thousand souls saved and then fifty million. Is it business that is coursing through you? Is it books, or songs, or inventions? Whatever you are called and destined to do, whatever your purpose is, it should not only be fruitful, it should multiply.

Why do you have a hard time believing this? Why do you not believe that you could have a multimillion dollar business, or write multiple books, or expand your agency to multiple programs? There are others out there, most of whom are not even Christians, who believe enough to walk in this blessing. They believe they can multiply and become great. God is trying to get us to see that we walk under the same blessing, and whoever embraces it will become great. If you don't want to become many or become numerous for yourself, then do it to make God look good. Embrace it, and accept it for His Glory. That's a better reason anyway. It is to the glory of God that we take what He has given us and give it back to Him increased and great. So *rabah*! Multiply and become great, become many, and become much.

BECOME MUCH

The word *rabah* is also translated to be, or to become much, to make much, or to do much. It is unacceptable to live in laziness, complacency, and apathy. You have a blessing on you to become much, to make much, and to do much. *Rabah*! What is in you that you are supposed to become?

Think of a new born baby boy. There is a man in him. You don't see it yet. The baby can't talk, can't walk, and can't eat on his own. He has little bitty feet, tiny hands, a button nose, and a small mouth. But, there is a blessing on the baby that gives him the capacity to grow and though he is not a man yet, there is a man in him. He cannot stay little. He has to become much. What is in him right now is a little bit of a man, but he is to become much of a man.

What is in you a little that is supposed to become much? Is there a preacher in you? Is there a teacher, intercessor, business woman, writer, singer, builder, property mogul, prophet, or administrator? Then it is time for you to become much, to make much, and to do much. You are not supposed to end your life little.

In effect, *rabah* places the same blessing over you that Christ put on the two fish and five loaves of bread. It was a little, but when Jesus blessed it, (and he may have even said "*rabah*, multiply!") it became much, it made much, and it did much. It fed 5,000 men plus women and children. You may feel like two fish and five loaves of bread, but God's word commands you to *rabah*! Multiply! Do much! Get up and walk under this blessing and find something to do. Find that thing you were born and created to do. Don't leave this world having done only a little when you have been blessed to do much. The biggest fear in my life used to be the fear of not being enough, and therefore, not doing much with my life. But, the bigger fear was what if I did have enough, and still failed to do something significant with my life. We all have the blessing to become much. It will look differently on all of us because we have differing gifts, but all the gifts were designed to *rabah*!

INCREASE YOUR INCREASE

Rabah also means increase. Now this is interesting because *parah* also can be translated increase. So *parah, rabah* could mean increase, increase! What was God's intent in pairing these two words together? The answer is in the translation to the English; be fruitful and multiply. *Parah* is increase by addition. *Rabah* is increase by multiplication. First, God gave us the ability to add. Then, He came right back and gave us the capacity to multiply.

If you will do the work to produce whatever it is that your purpose dictates you to produce, God will look at what you produced and give it the capacity to multiply. In other words, the blessing we are under increases our increase.

We have the capacity to proclaim and experience this blessing in every area of our lives. I have to get my finances under this blessing! I need my ministry, my investments, my books, my leadership, my sermons, and everything God has given me the ability to produce, under this blessing, so that when I see some fruitfulness, right after that, I will see some multiplication. I don't have to work it so hard because the Word works it for me. *Rabah*!

THRIVE: LONG, TALL AND LARGE

Now just like we found with the word *parah*, *rabah* has a qualitative, as well as a quantitative, aspect. *Rabah* is also translated long, tall, and large. This is more of an accurate translation when the word is used toward plant life. The crop, or plant, being blessed gained the capacity to grow long, tall and large. When put together, *parah* can mean to grow, and *rabah* can mean long, tall and large. So *parah*, *rabah* can be translated grow long, tall and large. It is the quality of what is being blessed. You don't just want a lot of weak, pitiful stuff produced by your gifts. What you produce is supposed to flourish—that is *parah*; but, it also must thrive—that is *rabah*.

We are under a blessing that gives us the capacity to thrive. The quality of your product should be excellent. Whatever is surging in you to produce has a blessing on it that makes it not only abundant, but of excellent quality. We serve a God of excellence. We should praise Him according to His excellent greatness. Our life, and what we do with the gifts that He placed in us, is our praise to God. We glorify Him when we become excellent in what He created us to do. He has empowered us to produce in a way that praises Him according to His excellent greatness.

All of our stuff should be great stuff. Our worship services should be great services. Our businesses, and the products they produce, should be of excellent quality. Every book we write, and every song we sing, should be great to the best of our ability. Proclaim this blessing over your children, your family, your marriage, and your home. *Rabah*! Thrive! Thrive like a long, tall and large plant. *Rabah* has a spirit of excellence in it. It commands us to multiply, to become great, to become many, to be much, to make much, to do much, to increase your increase, and to thrive.

MULTIPLY IN NUMBER AND STATUS

Lastly, *rabah* can be translated to mean to multiply in number and status. This is the same principle. It speaks to quantity and quality. The Bible says, in Deuteronomy 28, that the blessing of God makes us the head and not the tail, above only and not beneath. In everything you do, there should be an eventual increase in status. We are not to just be big ballers, but we are to be the shot callers as well. We should rise to the top of whatever we pursue. Again, with this kind of blessing over your life, why are you not doing big things? You have to believe it, declare it, and get after it. You have to get up, grow up and go up to be what is in you to be. The blessing has already been spoken over your life as a created man, or woman of God, and especially as a restored, born-again, child of God.

In the parable of the prodigal son, the father restored his repentant son to the status he had before he left his father's house. We are the son in that story, and God is the Father. When we repented, He restored us to our original blessing. That blessing was spoken over us in Eden. Jesus, the last Adam, restored for us what we lost in the first Adam. Jesus said Himself that it was the Father's good pleasure to give us the Kingdom. I don't believe that humankind ever lost this five-fold blessing, but even if we did, it has been restored in Jesus Christ. Let's get back to Eden and live under our original blessing for the glory of God!

Rabah! Multiply. Increase, grow great, thrive, and grow long, tall and large. Multiply in quality, quantity, and status. Be fruitful—*parah*. Multiply—*rabah*. Fill to capacity—*male*.

CHAPTER 3

Male! Fill to Capacity

And God blessed them, and God said unto them, "Be fruitful (*parah*), and multiply (*rabah*) and replenish the earth (*male*)..."

In the beginning, God created the heavens and the earth, but something happened after that. Some Bible scholars believe it was the war between God and Lucifer, and the earth somehow got destroyed. Whatever the reason, the second verse of the Bible says "the earth was without form and void." It was formless and empty—an empty waste. The earth was lifeless and barren. Nothing was going on here. The earth was space on which nothing was living, breathing, or having activity. It was capacity with no productivity.

Then, God creates life in a small space on this vast planet. He creates us and puts us in the small space. Then, He looks at the large space and says *parah*! Be fruitful! Be productive! Increase! Grow! Branch off! Flourish! Produce offspring of the same kind in abundance! Then, God says *rabah*! Multiply! Become great! Become many! Be much! Make much! Do much! Increase your increase! Thrive! Increase in number and status!

Then, God says *male* (pronounced maw-lay) which is translated in the King James Version of the Bible as "replenish the earth." More clearly, it is translated "fill the earth to capacity." *Male* gives purpose to *parah* and *rabah*. *Parah* and *rabah* are the what. *Male* is the *what for*. God is a God of purpose, and every *what* has a *why*. Every *what* has a *what for*. Be fruitful and multiply so that you can replenish this earth and fill it to capacity. Adam and Eve were blessed with the ability to produce and reproduce and become great. They were released to do much, to be much, to flourish, to increase and to do it abundantly. Every one born from them has the same blessing. Of course, the entrance of sin into the world complicated it, perpetrated it, and perverted it. But, Jesus solved the sin issue at the cross, so let's get back to our original blessing. Let's get back to Eden. So *male*! Fill your life...fill your space...to capacity.

You have been given space in the form of life, time, potential, and location. God has given each of us these four precious gifts. God has given you life! Then, He gave you time. None of us know how much exactly, but we do have some time. Then, He places in each of us different levels of potential. These are the gifts, talents, tendencies, and instincts we have toward certain activities or purposes. It is that which is surging in us that is supposed to bring forth fruit. We all have individual potential. He then places us in a location on this earth. It was preordained that you were born where you were born, and that you settled where you settled. That is your location. So, we have been given space in terms of life, time, potential, and location.

LIFE AND TIME

Let's combine the first two—life and time. What are you going to do with your lifetime? The blessing says I can take this lifetime and fill it to capacity. Life and time are incredible gifts of God. He expects us to take advantage of these gifts He has given us, and do something with our lifetime that has eternal impact. Even if it's just for this world, let your lifetime have impact on someone, on some community, or on some issue. What are you doing with your lifetime? So many people die young, never having the opportunity to reach their potential. But, here you are with another day, another moment, and perhaps another year, or another decade. What are you going to do with the time you have left? What will you do with your lifetime?

POTENTIAL AND LOCATION

Then add the other two—potential and location. We have a blessing on us that gives us the ability in our lifetime to use our potential to fill a specific location to capacity. For example, imagine someone has bought a building. They walk into that particular location with life, time and potential. Their job is to use that potential to fill the building to capacity with whatever they are gifted to produce. If they make furniture, and plan to make it and sell it out of this location, they start with one piece and keep making furniture until they have filled the location to capacity.

You are gifted to produce something. You have been given the life and time to be fruitful. But, God placed you in a particular location to fill it up with the fruit of your potential. Your space may be a classroom, or a business, or a factory, or a church. Your space may be the city, or the small community you live in. You are to fill that place to capacity. God has given you space in which to be blessed, and that space is given in terms of life, time, potential, and location. *Male!*

Another example is the World Wide Web. It wasn't a physical space. It was an idea of space whose capacity was every computer in the world. Someone with life and time saw the potential of being able to connect computers all over the world. There was location in cyberspace and they have filled it! That is *male*.

REPLENISH

We have the ability to build, or rebuild anything we put our hands to. If something was built or established, and then destroyed, we have a blessing on us that gives us the ability to rebuild things again. It was there, something happened, and we can get it there again. Because this word is translated "replenish," there is an indication that the earth was in good shape originally. There are some who, by putting several scriptures together, assert that Lucifer, Satan's original angelic name, had some kind of dominion in the earth. When he got caught up in pride, he fought against God. In his defeat, what he had dominion over was destroyed. God then created humankind, and gave us this earth, and told us to replenish it. He told us to repopulate it and to build it back up.

This entire account may or may not be factual, but what I want you to see is that there is a builder in you. There is replenisher in you. Whether it is a business, a marriage, a ministry, a family, an agency, or an institution, you can *male*. You can replenish it. Don't be intimidated by any job, task, call, or responsibility. God has given you the capacity and the ability to replenish. You don't have to settle for a life torn apart. You don't have to settle for a marriage that is only a shadow of the joy it used to be. You don't have to give in to despair when your family becomes dysfunctional. You don't have to endure the decline of a ministry or business. Before God gave us this earth, it was without form and void. It was empty and barren. He started the process and turned it over to us, and we have replenished it. We have repopulated it. We have built it back up. Of course, there was a word from God and His creative power, but the replenishing was up to us. What a team we make with God! We are still a great team, especially those of us who are born again to work with Him on His agenda for the world. God starts it off with His word. We *male*.

FILL TO CAPACITY

A better translation of the word *male* is to fill, to fill up a space, to fill to capacity, to be full, or simply fullness. Humankind was given this earth and placed in a small garden. However, there was so much earth to be filled. God saw the end result as the earth being populated. He saw towns and cities and kingdoms. He saw families and tribes and nations. So He blessed humankind, and said to them, *male!* Fill this earth to capacity.

Now you have been given life, time, potential, and location. Have you filled your life to capacity? Are you capable of more than what you are doing? Have you done as much ministry as you have been given space to do? Have you generated as much income as you have the capacity to generate? Have you written as much as you can? Have you spoken as excellently as you can? Have you learned as much as you are capable of learning, or done as much as you are capable of doing? Have you parented as well, loved as hard and as much, or grown as great as you have been given life, time, potential, and location to do?

If you have more room in your life to fill, then you need to declare to yourself, *male!* You aren't done yet! You have more space. You have more life. You have more potential. There are more ideas in you. There is more ability and more capacity in you. You aren't done yet! If you have another year of health and more dreams that have not yet been fulfilled, then you aren't done yet. If God is still speaking to you about your future, and you can see things in your spiritual eye that your natural eye has not yet seen, then you aren't done yet. I have heard many global leaders say that each of us should die empty. They say we should pour out of us all that we are capable of. I don't know if that is possible, but I do know that every day, we should be striving to give back to God something for His investment in us. If there is more in you, and you have the health and mental capacity to get to it, then you are not done yet. *Male!*

FINISH IT!

Male also means be accomplished, be ended, be complete, and be finished. God stood over the man and woman He made and spoke the word *male*. In other words, finish this thing! Accomplish this, and end it up right. Complete what you were created to do. You will be fruitful and multiply until you have filled this earth to capacity, and then look back and say, it is finished. There is nothing more to do. I filled up my space. I accomplished my task. I completed my work. I worked it until it was ended. I am finished.

Jesus tells a story about a man who left his servants with talents to invest while he was gone. When the master returns, the two servants who doubled their money by working it and investing it heard him say "well done." The Christian world (at least in my culture) took that parable, especially the words "well done", and made it the focus of eulogies, songs, and celebrations. Growing up, I would often hear adults say, "I just want to hear Him say 'well done.'" It is the ultimate compliment from God. It means God is pleased with your life. It means you get to go to heaven. It means you will receive your heavenly reward.

We used the phrase as if it were one word. It was used like a compound word with one meaning. But, God had me to look at the words separately—well and done. Not only does this speak to the quality of what the servants did, it also speaks to the finality of what they did. Not only was the final result *well*, it was also *done*. God began to talk to me about the word *done*. When we see God face to face, as we are invited into eternity, I don't just want to hear the word *well*. I want Him to be able to say *done*! I want to know that I finished it; that I completed what God assigned me to do in this world. Because I love Him, I want Him to be pleased with me. When I close my eyes in physical death, I want to be done. Before Jesus closed His eyes in physical death, He was able to say to His Father, "it is finished." I am striving to be like Jesus. And to help me along, God has spoken this blessing—this capacity, this ability—over my life. *Parah*! *Rabah*! *Male*! Be fruitful and multiply and fill to capacity until you are done.

You don't have to settle for a life half-done. God is saying to someone reading this book that you have not done nearly what was possible with the space He gave you. But, you still have this blessing on you. All you have to do is get to it. If God has given you the responsibility, then you have the ability to *male*. Finish the thing! If He has given you the vision to do it, then you have the internal and external provision to do it. So replenish, build it up, fill it, fulfill it, complete it, accomplish it, and finish it. You're not done yet!

OVERFLOW AND ABUNDANCE

Finally, the word has also been translated to have a quantity of space filled with a mass, with a collection, with an overflow, or with abundance. Humankind was to take this earth, this quantity of space, and fill it with a mass, or a collection of things. It was supposed to be filled completely until there was such an abundance there would be overflow. Whatever it is you are supposed to do, then do a lot of it. Put in the work on your gift, talent, or ability until there is overflow and abundance. Whatever it is you are supposed to be, then be that to the maximum level. Be the best that is in you to be. Know it well. Be the expert.

If you are a writer, don't stop at just one book, one collection of poems, or just the plays you write for the church. If you are to sing, don't settle for a slot every third Sunday of the month. If you are called to be a preacher, do more than wait for your turn at your local church. If you are to serve, learn how to do more than one job. If you are to raise children, decide to be the best parent you have ever met. Read, learn, and be the expert. Teach others how to do what you did. If you are to be in business, make it your goal to expand and corner the market, if God gives you that vision. If you are to build an agency, make sure that it is the premier agency in your city. Strive to ensure that no one does it better and the clients come running to you until you have no more space or time. Whatever it is, do it until there is overflow and abundance.

Male! Replenish, fill to capacity, complete it, accomplish it, finish it, and do it in abundance. Do it in your life time, with your potential, and in the location God has given you. Fill up your space. Whatever you are supposed to accomplish, do it until it is done. Whatever space God gives you, fill it to capacity. Don't let your best gifts die in you. *Male*!

CHAPTER 4

Kabash! Subdue

And God blessed them, and God said unto them, "Be fruitful (*parah*), and multiply (*rabah*), and replenish the earth (*male*), and subdue it (*kabash*)…"

God knew when He blessed us to be fruitful and multiply and fill our world to capacity that our world was not always going to cooperate. He told Adam and Eve to go out there and subdue the earth. The Hebrew word is *kabash*. This is the first indication, in this five-fold blessing, that there may be some difficulty and challenge that comes with being blessed. We are not going to go out there and be fruitful, and multiply, and fill to capacity without experiencing some difficulty. If you are going to *parah*, *rabah*, and *male*, God seems to be saying that you better know how to *kabash* as well.

When you increase, decrease is waiting around the corner. When you become great, you also become a target. There is a weight that comes with glory. There are some growth pains that come with productivity. Responsibility is the consequence of prosperity. When you branch off there also has to eventually be some pruning. You are going to need to develop some management skills when you are being much and doing much.

As you begin to produce and become great and increase your increase, you have to be careful to not let your world go wild and get away from you. Being blessed brings with it serious issues. Some issues will come with the growth and prosperity itself. Other issues will come with your own failure to keep up. Some will come from just life on planet earth, and some will come from the enemy (the devil).

But God has already given us the capacity to get it all under control and make it work the way it is supposed to work. *Kabash*! Subdue your world! You have to have the attitude that this is my world. God gave it to me. He put me in charge and it's my world. I don't have to give up on my dream. I don't have to downsize my vision. I don't have to play down my ambition, or settle for less than what I see in my future. This is my world, and I have been blessed to subdue it. *Kabash*!

BRING INTO SUBJECTION

Kabash is to bring something into subjection. It means forced submission to control by another. It means to be under the power or authority of another. Your personal world, and everything in it, is supposed to be under your authority, under your control, and under your power. So I ask you this question:

What in your world is running wild? What in your world is not doing what you want it to do?

When it comes to your financial situation, is your spending under control? Is your income being used in a manner that you have total control over? How are things on your job? Are you in balance, or are you overwhelmed? Do you control your schedule, or does your schedule run wild with you? Are your thoughts under control, or does your mind wander constantly, refuse to shut down at night, or keep jumping from topic to topic and thought to thought all day? What about your emotions, your eating habits, your time, or your body? What in your life is running wild? Is your marriage on a roller coaster? Are your children acting as if they are on their own?

If there is anything in your world that is running wild and is not in submission to what you want, then you are not walking in this blessing. Is your life defying your authority? Then this book is coming to remind you that you have been given the capacity to bring it into subjection by force. You have the ability to get back into control in every area of your life that God has given you dominion over. Of course, there are some things in life none of us can control. In and of ourselves, we control very little of anything. But, when God gives us the authority over our world, then we can subdue it. We can bring it under the power and authority God has ordained for us to have.

How do I do that? First you have to believe that the power of the God that spoke this word over your life makes you more powerful than anything else in your world. When you know that you are bigger and stronger than the opposition, you get out there and use force. For example, if a two-year-old, or a puppy dog is running around your house tearing things up, you go grab them, and hold them, and make them stop their behavior by force. You know you are bigger. You know you are more powerful, and you know how to bring them into subjection. You subdue them.

The same is true for whatever is running wild in my life. I know I am bigger and more powerful than that thing. I'm bigger than my money, my body, my marriage, and my mind. I am more powerful than my habit, my work situation, my poor time management, and my selfish will. I know that I am bigger and stronger, so now I just have to figure out to bring it down. You bring down wild money management differently than you bring down a wild appetite. If lust is running wild in your life, there is a different strategy than if work is not doing what you need it to do.

There are several places you can go to find out how to bring areas of your life under subjection. Some of the strategies will only be found in prayer. For some of these areas, you are going to need counseling. You can find the answers in books on the subject, and especially in *the* book called the Holy Bible. The Bible is full of the stories of people who have brought down things in their lives that were defying their God given authority. Noah subdued the flood by the strategy of building a protective ark. Joshua subdued Jericho by obeying God's instruction to march and make some noise. David subdued Goliath by not conforming to accepted war tactics, and instead, using what he was proficient in. Solomon subdued his kingdom with wisdom while Jehoshaphat subdued his with prayer.

I could go on and on into the New Testament and talk about Jesus subduing the storm by His Word, and the Apostles subduing problems in a growing church by appointing deacons. I'm sure in your church, and in your family, there are people who stand as examples of how to bring things back into order and under authority. Whatever in your life is out of control, you must know that there is a way to bring it into forced submission. Some of us went through it so we can tell you how to do it.

In the movie Independence Day, the United States military, with the help of a computer engineer, were the first to figure out how to defeat the alien army who was about to invade the entire earth. The aliens had already attacked major cities all over the globe. The Americans, through much trial and error, finally figured out how to destroy their mother ship and then all of their other ships that were stationed worldwide and ready to invade. Once the Americans disoriented the mother ship and got the force fields to malfunction, they were able to successfully take down one of the other ships. At that point, the Chief of Staff said to his men who were sending Morris code, "tell them how to bring the bastards down boys." Later, the response came back to him, "they are coming down all over the world!"

Well, I declare to you, your independence day! *Kabash*! Bring every wild thing in your life under subjection. Wild things are coming down all over the Kingdom of God because this blessing is still in effect over humankind. If anything in your life is not doing what you want it to do, you have the ability to bring it into subjection. Find the right strategy and bring them down.

KEEP UNDER

Kabash also means to keep under subjection. The subjection is not temporary. Once you have something under control, you keep it under submission to your authority. You have a blessing on you that says you don't have to be up and down. You do not have to be unstable and at the mercy of the circumstances of your life. You can keep your life under subjection. This world was never to overtake us. We were designed to overtake it and keep our position on top. The world does not live on top of us. According to the blessing that Moses declared for those who obey God, "the Lord will make you the head and not the tail…you will always be at the top, never at the bottom." (see Deuteronomy 28)

When you get on top of your finances, stay there. When your health is finally under control, keep it there. When you get some stability in your mental status, you are to hold on to your sanity. Whether it is your family life, your ministry, your physical body, or your habits, you have the ability to keep under control that which you have brought into subjection. *Kabash!* Keep that wild stuff under, and you stay on top of it. This is your world—subdue it!

BRING INTO BONDAGE OR ENSLAVE

You are the master—your body is the slave. You are the master—your time is the slave. You are the master—your appetite is the slave. You are the master—your emotions, your money, your business are all the slaves. Bondage means that the thing you have subdued is under restriction. When something is bound, it does not have the ability to move freely. It is restricted. There should not be anything in your world that does not have restrictions.

Sexually, there should be some things you do not do. Of course, the Bible teaches that there should be no sexual intercourse outside of marriage, but even if you decide to break God's law, hopefully there are some people you would never consider touching. Even in marriage, there should be some boundaries you never cross. Nutritionally, there should be some things you do not eat for health reasons. Behaviorally, you should have some things that are out of the question for you to do. Emotionally, there should be some restrictions on your anger, or anxiety, or even celebration. Socially, there are some places you should refuse to go, some activities you refuse to participate in, some things you refuse to drink, and some people you do not associate with. Financially, there needs to be a budget and some restriction on your spending. You should always have money somewhere that you do not spend. Even spiritually, there should be a balance in your life with other natural activities you need to attend to. There should be nothing in your life that does not have restrictions.

Put your world on restriction. *Kabash*! Your world has been given to you, and you need to bring it into bondage under your godly wisdom and authority. Subdue your world. Bring everything connected to you under control. Tell everything in your world, "You are not going to do everything you want to do when you want to do it. You have some restrictions." Nothing in your life should be running wild. Nothing in your life should be out of control. Treat yourself, and all that concerns you, like you treat a child who has broken the house rules. When you overeat on Monday, tell your body on Tuesday that "you're on restriction." When you overspend in January, tell your pocketbook and your debit card that, "you're on restriction for the month of February." When your time management is unmanaged, remember that you have a blessing on you that can pull things together, subdue them, and keep them under control.

TREAD DOWN BY FORCE

Another translation of the word *kabash* is to tread down by force. The image is to chase that thing that is wrecking your life and walk on it, walk over it, and press it beneath your feet. This is the same concept as keeping it under, but much more forceful. Sometimes *kabash* is not a particularly nice word. It is used for things that get in the way of *parah*, *rabah*, and *male*. Be fruitful, and multiply, and fill your world to capacity, and if anything gets in your way, if anything refuses to cooperate, or if anything gets out of control—subdue it. Tread it down by force! If it does not fit, force it.

If it's in your life, and it does not fit your life's call, then force it. If it does not fit into your dream, then tread it down and force it to conform. If it does not fit the vision of what God said about you, or who you are in Christ, then it must be subdued, chased down, and tread down by force. Get aggressive with the things that are coming against the well-being of your life. If it does not fit, go after it aggressively. Do not passively let things run wild in your life. Do not be overwhelmed by anything that feels out of control.

Look at your life and make an assessment. This habit doesn't fit with my call (what God wants me to do). This lust doesn't fit my anointing (the free flow of the power of God and His approval). This money situation doesn't fit my vision (what God has revealed to me). This health situation doesn't fit my dream. This mindset doesn't fit who I am in God. So I have to *kabash* it, subdue it, and tread it down by force. You have the power and the authority to bring your world under subjection. Again, there are so many different ways to do this depending on what it is that is out of control. Be aggressive. Find a strategy. Be radical about it. If it doesn't fit into the God-given direction for your life, it cannot be allowed to have an unrestricted presence in your world. *Kabash!*

OVERCOME, CONQUER AND CONTROL AN ENVIRONMENT

It is your world. God gave it to humankind, and He gave your part of this world to you when He supplied you with life, time, potential, and location. Nothing in your world should overcome you. You are to overcome, conquer, and control your world like Jesus did and as John declared:

> "I have told you these things, so that in me you may have peace. In this world you will have trouble. But take heart! I have overcome the world." (John 16:33 NIV)

> "You, dear children, are from God and have overcome them, because the One who is in you is greater than the one who is in the world." (1 John 4:4 NIV)

> "For everyone born of God overcomes the world. This is the victory that has overcome the world, even our faith. Who is it that overcomes the world? Only the one who believes that Jesus is the Son of God." (1 John 5:4, 5 NIV)

When Jesus overcame and conquered this world, He gave us back the ability to live fully and completely under the original blessings: *parah, rabah, male, kabash, radah*. Be fruitful, and multiply, fill your world to capacity, subdue it, and have dominion. If there is anything running wild in your world, or is totally out of control, or is working against your authority, you have the capacity to *kabash*!

Subdue it, stay on top of it, bring it under subjection, keep it under, enslave it, put it on restriction, tread it down, overcome and conquer it. Do it now. Do it here. Make that first step with the authority of the words of your mouth. Speak to those areas. Pray, decree and declare that your appetites, your emotions, your behaviors, your finances, your family life, and your habits are all coming under control in the Name of Jesus. Then find those strategies in the Bible, in books, in counseling, or with a mentor or coach that will bring those things under subjection, and keep them there. The blessing on your life, spoken by God the day humankind was created, gives you the power, the permission, and the authority to *kabash*! Walk in that authority. Believe it and act on it. Just like back in Eden, you are to live on top of your world.

CHAPTER 5

Radah! Have Dominion

And God blessed them, and God said unto them, "Be fruitful (*parah*), and multiply (*rabah*), and replenish the earth (*male*), and subdue it (*kabash*) and have dominion (*radah*) over the fish of the sea, and over the fowl of the air, and over every living thing that moveth upon the earth." (Genesis 1:27, 28 KJV)

We were created to live on top of the world. We were created to be in control. We were placed on this planet to be the managers of life. So, I encourage you to *radah*—to have dominion. Do not shy away from your assignment. You were created to have dominion. You were blessed to have dominion. You are still living under that blessing in Christ Jesus.

To review, after we were given the capacity to be fruitful and multiply, to *parah* and *rabah*, we were given the ability to *male*—fill up our space to that capacity. Then, we were empowered to get what we produced under subjection when it begins to grow out of control—to subdue it or *kabash*. Now, we have to manage it. We have to keep it under control while letting it continue to grow. This is the Hebrew word *radah*.

There is a narrow difference between *kabash* and *radah*. Let me explain it this way. Say you have a dog that is running wild. It is tearing up your home, running in the street, getting too far away from the house, and digging holes all over the neighborhood. You chase it down, grab it, get it under control, hold it tight, and stop it from expressing itself all over the place. You have subdued the dog. That is *kabash*. But, you have to let a dog be a dog. The dog needs to grow, develop, move, and do what it is designed to do. There has to be away to let the dog continue to thrive without letting the dog get out of control again. So, you put the dog on a leash so that it can have some expression, but now you have the ability to pull it back, make it go left or right, or forward and then stop.

In the same way, after we get life under control, we have to, in a sense, put a leash on it. This is the meaning of the word *radah*. We are to have dominion over the things that we subdue. The blessing is designed to keep on blessing us. It has to be allowed to do what it was designed to do. We are designed and blessed to be fruitful and to constantly produce. When that production gets out of control, it must be subdued, but not stopped to the point that there is never any more production. It has to be managed. We have dominion. We are the rulers of the earth. Humankind is to manage everything we see and everything we have.

Take your finances, for example. God blesses you to make

some money, then increase it, and then use it to fill up your life. For most of us, at some time, it gets out of control, so we stop everything so we can manage it. This $1,000 will go here. That $500 goes there. The other $10,000 will stay over there. You put a leash on it.

Your body should be under your dominion. You feed it, and it grows. It increases. It is supposed to do just that. It was designed fill itself to capacity, but then gets out of control and you are overweight. You now have to stop your body from growing any further. You subdue it, but you still have to eat, so now you *radah*. You manage your body and have dominion over it. You tell your body, "no, you can't have that, but you can have this; not at this time, but that time is okay." You have been given free will and dominion to make your life what you want it to be.

After you *kabash*, you have to *radah*. After you subdue your world, you are to have dominion. You are to manage and handle the business of your world. You are blessed to be able to make your world do what it was designed to do in an orderly, efficient, and effective manner. *Radah*!

DOMINATE

The word *radah* means to dominate, to have a commanding influence over, to exercise control over, and to rule by superior authority or power. When God made humankind, male and female, He set us in this earth and gave us dominion over everything else He made—everything we could see.

No matter what happens, we will always be on top of the animal world. There are those who do not believe that. They believe we all evolved, and man is just the highest evolved creature. As time goes on, they believe it is possible that another animal may become more evolved than humankind. The Bible teaches that humankind was formed in God's image and in God's likeness and was given dominion over everything else God created. We will reign in the earth until the end of time. We have been given the ability and the capacity to dominate everything on this earth.

Whatever we imagine, we will eventually do. We have a blessing on us that gives us the capacity to eventually dominate it. We saw cheetahs moving fast, and we figured out how to move faster. We saw the stingray and dolphins speeding through water, and we created a way to do it better. We saw the birds flying, and we figured out how to do it more efficiently. We can do anything they can do, but they can't do what we do because we have been blessed to have dominion.

We have a commanding influence over our world. We can change the natural order of things. We can add to our abilities and influence the abilities of the animal and plant kingdom. Although it is not a good thing, we have most likely even affected our weather. We have been given a commanding influence over our world, so don't let your world have a commanding influence over you.

Don't let circumstances back you up. Don't let situations back you down. Man up! Woman up! Realize that you have dominion. Stop being a victim of circumstance. Stop making excuses. Stop being the weakest link. Walk in the power and authority of the original blessing and *radah*. You are to use your God given authority to dominate the physical and spiritual world around you. You have the authority of the Name of Jesus to change and manage things in your world. As long as your will is lined up with the will of God, and you do nothing that undermines His authority, you can speak to your world and expect it to eventually respond. To be honest, even when humankind works against God, He will typically let us have what we choose. The evidence is in the condition of our world at this very moment. Most of the things that are going on are because of what we chose, and not from what He would have chosen for us if we, as human beings, had continued to honor His commands. He turned this world over to us, for the good or the bad. He will judge in the end, but for now we have the blessing on us to dominate this earth. We have dominion.

RULE AND REIGN

The word *radah* indicates long-term leadership. You are to have a continuing leadership over your life and everything in your life. *Radah* means to reign and to rule. Humankind was appointed by God to reign and rule over the earth under His authority. As an extension of that authority, we are to first rule our own lives. To rule means to be out front making decisions and expecting results. That's what a ruler does. A ruler makes decisions and expects results.

Make a decision not to be financially unstable all of your life and expect results. Make a decision to get a college degree and expect the result. Make a decision to own your own home, or be healthy, or have a good marriage, or be an excellent parent—and expect results. You have been blessed to rule and reign. You are not just to look around hoping and waiting to see what happens next. You take responsibility. You make a decision and expect results. Do what you need to do to get things done in your life. You have been created to have dominion. Start with your own world. Rule and reign in your world. Take responsibility over your own life and look for your life to produce the results you are looking for.

Assume the position of authority in your world. You are the master of your fate. You are the captain of your soul. As the poem by English poet William Ernest Henley says:

> It matters not how strait the gate
> How charged with punishments the scroll
> I am the master of my fate
> I am the captain of my soul.

This, in no way, undermines the authority of God or the reality of His sovereignty. Yes, there are more things in life you cannot control than there are things you have absolute control over. But, it was God who spoke the words over humankind and gave them dominion over the earth. You cannot control the things that only God can control, but you do have the ability to take authority over how you respond to those things and how you make them fit in to what you have decided for your life.

PREVAIL AND GOVERN

Radah also means to prevail and govern with considerable forceful authority. This suggests that staying on top of your world might be a fight. Your life is going to put up a fight. The devil, the haters, and the betrayers are going to put up a fight. Your own weakness and sinful nature is going to put up a fight. You have to prevail. You will have to use forceful authority and get rough with it sometimes. We don't do it with carnal, worldly or natural weapons. We do it with spiritual weapons. We do the spiritual warfare that casts out demons and cancels their assignments against us. We war against our own weaknesses by fasting and prayer and disciplining our bodies. We fight against being overwhelmed by others, who do not want our success, by being tenacious and uncompromising and by ending those relationships when necessary.

We have dominion. Whatever we bind on earth will be that which has been bound in heaven, and whatever we loose on earth will be that which has been loosed in heaven (see Matthew 18). In other words, what God has declared to be true in the heavens, He has given us the authority to declare and bring to fruition on the earth. Don't let life intimidate you. Don't let problems discourage you. Don't let your circumstances overwhelm you, and don't let trouble wear you down. Don't run from your assignment and responsibilities, whether they be marriage, or family, or ministry, or business.

Radah! Prevail and govern it with forceful authority and have dominion. No matter what happens, you will always end up on top because God has blessed you to be in charge. So, don't be afraid to wrestle things down that rise up against you, and your dream, and your vision. Get back out there and fight until you prevail. Do not let life get the best of you. You have dominion.

DIRECT

You get to choose the direction of your life. This doesn't mean that you don't pray and ask God for direction. But, once you have His approval and He has given you the go ahead, you are to direct your life. When God spoke the word *radah*—have dominion—He put us in charge to direct this world and lead it into the direction He placed before us. Our purpose in this earth is to direct it. We are the only ones in the earth that have the power to move it into the right direction. And again, I am encouraging you to start with your own world.

Think of it as being the co-star of your own movie, and you are the director as well. If you don't like it, change it. If you don't like the way you look, or the career you have chosen, or the way your marriage works, or the atmosphere at your job, then change it. If you don't like your financial situation, or the place that you live, or the way that you worship, then change it. You have been given the authority to be the director of this movie you call your life. God is the producer. He has given you the parameters, and the vision, and the way it should end. Then He handed you the script and made you the director. You have authority and using it is what it means to have dominion.

This became more apparent to me one night at Disneyland.

The show at the end of the day was called Fantasmic. In the show, Mickey Mouse is having a dream. A parade of Disney villains infiltrate his dream and make it a nightmare. Finally, Mickey Mouse had enough and said something so profound that it changed my perspective on my life. He said to the villains and the monsters and the dragon, "I know you think you're powerful, *but this is MY dream!*" And then, Mickey takes control and changes the direction of the dream. He decided that he was the director and that he had dominion.

TAKE INTO ONE'S OWN HAND

The word *radah* has its roots in a word that means to scrape out, scoop, grasp, or take with one's own hands. When it comes to the details of your life, you are to take them and put your blessed hands on them. The colloquial term "handle your business" is from this idea. Put your hands on whatever your heart tells you is your destiny to do. Grab it. Scoop it up. Scrape it out. Put your blessed hands on it. Like the first Psalm says, when you are a blessed person, everything you do will prosper. Take your life in your hands and manage it, work it, control it, put a leash on it, and make it do what it is supposed to do. If it puts up a fight and doesn't turn out the way you want it, then put your hands on it, scoop it up, grasp it, re-work it, make a decision about it and have dominion. Know that you have the words of your Creator God backing you up and giving you the power to bring your life into subjection and under your dominion. Do it now. Do it today. Take authority and have dominion. *Radah!*

EPILOGUE

Let's Get Back to Eden

So there you have it—the five original blessings that were spoken over humankind in the beginning. We were placed in the Garden of Eden with high hopes. We complicated things by disobeying God and handing our authority to Satan. We still had the blessing over us. We still were fruitful, and multiplied, and filled the earth. We still subdued the earth and had dominion over everything in it. Our dominion was complicated by our sins. We gave our authority to Satan, and even Jesus called him the god of this world. But the God-Man, Jesus Christ, won our place back, and as Christians, we of all people should walk under the original blessing.

This book comes to encourage you to begin walking in the faith of the original blessing over your life.

> Be fruitful and multiply—*parah, rabah*!
> Fill your world to capacity—*male*!
> Subdue whatever doesn't cooperate—*kabash*!
> Have dominion over it—*radah*!

There is a lifestyle that God has provided, that Jesus has purchased, and that the Holy Spirit is producing in all of us. So let's get back to Eden and live on top of the world. It is our world after all.

ABOUT THE AUTHOR

Dr. Naida M. Parson is a native of Las Vegas, Nevada and is the Senior Pastor of New Antioch Christian Fellowship. Dr. Parson is active in the community as a motivational speaker, writer, and mentor. She is a sought after Christian conference keynote speaker and the sole proprietor of A Way With Words LLC, which is the parent company for her speaking, writing, seminars, and training workshops. Dr. Parson is also a Certified Leadership trainer, coach, and speaker.

She holds a Bachelor of Arts Degree in Psychology and Black Studies from the University of California, Riverside. She has also earned a Master of Arts Degree in African-American Studies, with emphasis in Psychology from the University of California, Los Angeles, as well as, a Doctorate in Clinical Psychology from the University of Nevada, Reno. For over 30 years she has provided and coordinated mental health services for children, adolescents, adults and families.

She has been said to have a profound and creative "way with words" and has provided motivational speaking for several civil, corporate, and community organizations. She is well known for her ability to reach any audience regardless of age, gender, or cultural background. Her method of presentation causes her audience to look inward and leave the event with renewed enthusiasm and often a plan of action.

Printed in the United States
By Bookmasters